GET
NOTICED

GET
NOTICED

**HOW TO BOOST YOUR SMALL
BUSINESS PROFILE IN 30 DAYS OR LESS**

PAULA GARDNER

LEANMARKETING™
★PRESS★

First Published In Great Britain 2005
by Lean Marketing™ Press
www.leanmarketingpress.com

Typeset in Garamond and Humanist.

For Mum and Dad, and Joan –
who influenced me more than she realises

Acknowledgements

I'd like to take a moment to thank Gerry, for without him there wouldn't be a Get Noticed book; Heather Waring for her inspiration and motivation; Emily Gordon for her hard work and support; Chris and Hazel for their work on www.doyourownpr.com, and Joe, Debbie and Julie of Lean Marketing Press for making it all happen so smoothly.

Paula Gardner
www.doyourownpr.com

Contents

Introducing "Get Noticed!"

Congratulations! You've decided to invest the next 30 days in helping your business reach new heights.

PR is a fantastic source of free promotion. It can bring customers and clients to your door, and enhance your business reputation so that people are happier to pay more for your goods and services.

How cool is that?

And, let's be frank. It is quite simply a great kick to see your business profiled, whether it's in the *Huddersfield Echo* or the *Financial Times*.

This workbook is an invaluable kick start that will introduce you first hand to all that PR can do for you and your business success.

I am constantly amazed by clients who one day are celebrating a piece in their local newspaper and then just days later go on to appear in the *Daily Mail* or on *Radio 4*.

What's more, their growing excitement and enthusiasm is contagious. The boost to both you and your business profile can only be good for business.

I also like to think, "If they can do it, then you can do it too."

But to handle a PR campaign properly takes time. And, you don't need me to tell you, that for any small business time can be a very rare commodity.

That's why I decided to write this workbook. It will save you precious time (and money) by helping you focus on taking the actions that get results. I'll by pass all the fripperies and show you everything you need know to get the PR ball rolling and start benefiting from doing your own PR as you learn.

Clients and readers of my free newsletter *Get Noticed* (you can sign up via www.doyourownpr.com) have often told me how much they value my no nonsense action orientated approach. They are fed up with wading through pages of the author's thoughts and anecdotes before they can extract the right nugget of helpful information that they have been promised.

I've written this workbook in the same no nonsense way. The nuggets should be easy to find. We'll focus on taking action and getting results. Let's leave all the theory to the spectators!

These exercises will help you to form a PR campaign that will help you to raise your business profile. You'll also learn to become media savvy in a world where no business, large or small, can survive and grow without PR skills.

What's more these exercises can be done over and over again, either individually, when you feel that your PR needs a boost, or all together, when you would like to embark on another intensive campaign.

I have helped hundreds of businesses – from recruitment agencies to fashion designers, life coaches to IT providers – achieve and benefit from publicity.

Now it's your turn to get noticed!

Warm wishes,

Paula

Why Do Your Own PR In the First Place?
...and other frequently asked questions

I often get asked this question, and the answer is not always due to budget. For a start doing it yourself gives you control. Control over your image, control over your message and control over your time. Plus, nobody else is never going to know as much about your business as you.

And, once you've mastered the skills of PR by doing it yourself, if you do, at some point, employ someone else to do it for you, you'll know what they'll need to help you get noticed.

Other common questions are:

"How can I compete with the expertise and collective experience that a PR company can offer?"

Perhaps you can't, but if you are the only one with the expertise and experience of *your* company no one can do a better job of talking about it than you. To somebody working for a PR company your project may be just the means to a pay packet at the end of the month. But it's different for you; it's your livelihood. Who has the most motivation to do a great job? Who can bring the most enthusiasm and passion for your business to the job? Think about it.

"I'm shy. How on earth can I do PR?"

Ok, so you're not going to be serious competition for Absolutely *Fabulous'* Edina or a New Labour spin doctor but handling your own PR is a powerful confidence builder. If you're shy you're going to have to overcome some of your reserve. With confidence, comes competence, so the more you practice the better you get. More confidence is sure to help you with other aspects of your business too. And, if you really don't like the idea of coming out of your shell, you'll be glad to find there's a great deal that you can do using internet and email anyway.

"I really don't feel like wining and dining people just to get a story printed."

If you can provide a good story that will excite and enthuse a journalist then you won't need to wine or dine anybody. However, as you work on your PR campaign and come across journalists who show an interest in you and your work you'll begin to feel like cultivating them as useful contacts. This doesn't have to be in the form of wining and dining – there are plenty of other ways to nurture your relationships. A group business breakfast, a quick coffee or even arranging to meet at a trade conference or exhibition are just a few possibilities.

"I'll have to get to know so many publications and people; won't it be a full time job?"

One of the things you'll learn is how to focus and pin point your market, reducing the amount of potential contacts you'll need to get in touch with and being able to approach them with quality ideas, rather than sending out some random hit and miss press release to anyone with a pulse. As with most things, the *quality* of your approach and what you have to say is often more important than how many people you include in your mailout.

"Don't I have to be able to write well?"

I won't lie. Being able to write well does help. But you can always outsource your writing while retaining control over your PR. Alternatively, you could just get on the phone and talk to journalists – something we all too often forget about.

If you're able to write reasonably well then you should be fine. Journalists are more interested in a good story than they are in your grasp of English. So put together a press release that conveys what you need to say simply and without fuss. Forget flowery language and hype. The journalists have seen it all before a million times. Keep it simple and succinct.

"Aren't proper PR people going to have better contacts and access to magazines than me?"

Of course, the answer is yes. Professional PR people spend years building up contacts in lots of different publications and could probably reel off magazines and media outlets you wouldn't have dreamt of.

But the idea behind Doing Your Own PR is that you learn how to focus on the niche magazines, newspapers, websites, radio stations and TV programmes that your own personal customer base use and watch. You don't need extensive media contacts just the most appropriate ones.

Professional PR people work with a variety of clients, so they *need* to be aware of everyone from the latest teenage lyric printing magazine, to the driest columnist in a financial weekly.

You, however, have the luxury of being able to concentrate on those outlets that will benefit *you* the most. The number will be smaller, but hopefully the relationships you develop will be richer.

And no, it won't be a slap bang success at once. You will have to work hard at cultivating those contacts. But the beauty of it is that, once cultivated and nurtured, those contacts are yours, and not those of some PR person who can waltz off from their present agency to their new and better paid job leaving you right back where you started.

Never forget that however professional a PR person may be, and however many contacts they may have, they will never have *your* passion for *your* business – a passion that will hopefully be conveyed to the journalists and editors and inspire them to use your story!

About Paula Gardner and Do Your Own PR

I am a PR coach. I specialise in helping enthusiastic and proactive business owners raise their business profile in order to attract new customers and clients. Whether they want a short term boost to kick start their business or ongoing coaching and support, I can help.

My background is in writing and journalism. I had my first article published in Just Seventeen magazine at the age of 14 and moved into music PR in my twenties, attracted by the sheer glamour of working with celebrities like George Michael, Bananarama and Sonia (ooooh, see how that dates me).

Inevitably came the point (now 11 years ago) when I decided to set up in business on my own. The glamour suddenly came to an abrupt halt. The focus from that point on was on building a successful business and all the hard graft, sweat and tears that goes with it. But, despite the glamour and relative ease of being "employed" I'd never go back to working for someone else. Not now, Not ever!

So, I've been there. I've got my hands dirty. I know how frustrating it can be when you know you've created something good and yet, along with running your own business, you've still got to put in perhaps even more effort on PR ing and marketing it. And I'm a PR person!

But it can be extremely fun, exciting, and of, course rewarding. By doing your own PR you'll develop expertise in areas you perhaps never thought you'd ever have, together with skills that will benefit you both professionally and personally.

And, of course, you'll also benefit from watching your business grow from strength to strength. People will start to know who you are. Your business will certainly get noticed. Excited? Great! Let's get on with it.

How to Use This Workbook

This book contains 30 practical tasks for you to do with the emphasis very much on "doing" not just "reading". Completing each task will move you one step forward in your publicity endeavours. And, you'll start to benefit as you learn.

While some tasks are precise and focused on one particular action others are broader which will help you "think PR". This overview will put what you are doing into context and help you learn valuable skills that will stay with you, forever.

By allocating yourself daily sessions, you can work your way through the workbook and tasks in a way that will build a powerful overall PR machine in 30 days or less.

Or, alternatively, you can dip in and choose tasks that appeal to you at a particular time.

There is also space in this workbook for notes. Keeping notes will help you to chart your progress, and enable you to recall ideas, information and contacts that you can use again and again.

Day 1: Are you a Media Virgin or Media Pro?

We're going to begin by looking at your current foundations for PR.

Many of my clients come to me completely unaware of what media is out there and ready to be used. Some just have no interest in it (up until now), others just don't have the time to read, watch TV or listen to the radio, and a small number are just downright contemptuous about the media.

But for you, all that has got to stop.

So, let's examine your media knowledge.

Do you regularly read relevant trade and professional publications?

Are you aware of the differences between *The Sun* and *The Daily Telegraph*?

Or how about *The Guardian* and *The Daily Telegraph*?

Do you listen to the radio (and I don't mean music stations) and know which stations (and presenters) are respected for their thought provoking interviews? Are you familiar with your own (often overlooked) local or regional press?

I would like you to spend some time listing all the publications that you read, websites you visit on a regular basis and TV and radio shows you listen to. Once you've done that I'd like you to take a look at your list and put a tick next to those that you think are going to be relevant to your publicity campaign. You can disregard the rest.

The next step is to decide how *au fait* you are with these titles or shows. Do they need further action from you? If you get your copy of the trade magazine on a sporadic basis do you need to subscribe to it today? If so, do so. If you've got a pile of unread magazines that you should catch up with, then read those too.

Now, I'd like you to make a list of any publications that you are aware of, but don't read regularly, that you think could be relevant to your campaign. Decide what action you need to take on these. How many can you realistically read each week? Set yourself a goal to work through this list over the 30 days and promise to keep to it.

Summary

- List the media you know.
- List any action you need to take to get to know them better.
- List the media you think you should get to know.
- List the actions you need to take to get to know them better.

Day 1 Notes

Publications I know...	Action to Take...

Publications I know of...	Action to Take...

Day 2: Make A Date With Yourself

You run a business, right? So, how on earth are you going to fit in time to do this PR stuff?

Fitting PR in around your usual day to day schedule is probably the hardest thing that you are going to have to do in the course of this book. So let's make it easy. You need to carve out some regular time from your diary and allocate it towards working through these exercises. Book a meeting with yourself to do PR. And, just as you would with a client, stick to it and turn up on time!

Just as I never manage to get around to taking my Tae Bo and Latin American dancing lessons unless they are heavily underlined in my diary, likewise many of my clients never get down to doing PR unless they too have booked out blocks of time and made them sacrosanct.

My suggestion is to go through your diary for the next 30 days and find as many blocks of at least two hours together as you possibly can, at least twice a week.

If there isn't an obvious time slot for these exercises you'll need to look closely at what you are currently doing. What can you move/postpone/delegate or just forget about to make time for getting your business noticed?

Tools

There is space in this workbook for your own notes and ideas but you may also like to get yourself the following:

A thick notebook. A number of box files. A new address book for press contacts (you can do this on your PC if you wish but I always think it's handy to have in a paper format)

You will also need a guide to all the publications out there. In the UK The *Hollis* guide comes out twice a year and is currently £100 per issue, £165 for two. This has names and contact details for journalists on publications throughout the UK. You can buy it here: http://www.hollis pr.com/publications/mediaguide.htm

If you are on a tight budget the *Writers and Artists Yearbook* will give you a fair proportion of the contacts for a fraction of the cost. You should be able to purchase this at your local bookstore or you can buy online at www.amazon.co.uk.

If you're not in the UK then your own country should have a similar version of these. Check out a good bookstore for help.

Summary

- Allocate time.
- Gather together your PR tools.
- Buy your guide to publications.

Day 2 Notes

The times that I have set aside for my PR work are:

_____day, between _____and_____

_____day, between _____and_____

_____day, between _____and_____

or, alternatively, list the dates here:

Day Two Check List
- ☐ Notebook
- ☐ Box Files
- ☐ Address Book
- ☐ Writers and Artists Yearbook
- ☐ Hollis Directory

Day 3: Who Do You Want To Notice You?

Now we are going to pin point your target market.

You can waste a huge amount of time, effort and money on both PR and marketing if you don't who know you're trying to get noticed by. Anyone who has ever done a business plan will have sighed a "do I really have to?" when it came to the market research part, but this sort of investment of your time will save you hours and bring big rewards.

After all, why spend your precious time, effort and money getting great publicity in a magazine or newspaper that none of your customers and potential customers read?

Targeting past, present and potential clients is a great way to find out about their media preferences, and it's also a great excuse to remind them that you're still around at the same time.

The trick is to make a short and focused survey. Multiple choice questions, when applicable, have a much higher chance of being answered than questions that require the participant to ceate an answer out of thin air. If you can offer a little carrot as a reward for taking the time and effort to fill it in then your chances of a successful survey are even higher. Examples of a carrot could be a free ebook, entry into a competition, a free assessment or even a gift.

You can deliver the survey via post, email, or even as a pop up on your website.

If you know your survey participants well you could also conduct a telephone survey but remember, they're busy too so only do this if you know they're happy and able to help. In this scenario you are leaving yourself open to the sparks and ideas that can naturally occur in conversation: little gems such as "Oh, I saw a magazine the other day that looked interesting. I didn't pick it up but it's probably got a website...etc". These sort of things regularly crop up during conversations and you also get much more immediate feedback than you would with a written survey.

So, what do you need to know? For a PR survey you'll need to know some or a combination of the following, depending on your business:

➢ Age group
➢ What magazines and newspapers they read, (differentiate between fun and work, but remember you want both. Don't forget you can still target leisure publications and reach your potential clients when they are not working. A bit sneaky I know!)
➢ If these magazines have sections (such as the weekend broadsheets for instance) make sure you ask what part of the publication they read. After all one person reading *The Sunday Times* might read completely different sections to another person reading the same paper.
➢ What websites do they look at (again, both fun and work)?
➢ What radio stations do they listen to – and then what programmes? What presenters or interviewers do they rate? What TV programmes do they like to watch?
➢ How did they hear about you or your business in the first place? – so simple, and yet frequently unasked!

Once you've found the publications and types of media that make your customers tick you'll be able to concentrate on these and only these, saving you time, effort and lots of money!

Remember to always focus on getting noticed by the person who will pay for your product or service   even if they may not necessarily be the person who will be using them. For instance if you provide staff training then, of course you will be working with the staff of that company but it is the HR manager or Managing Director that you need to concentrate on in your survey; they are the decision makers and cheque writers.

Here is an example of a simple survey that I might use:

1. Age   20 29 ?   30 39 ?   40 49 ?   50 59 ?   60 plus ?

2. Gender   male ?   female ?

3. The Top 3 publications I read to keep on top in my work are…

4. The Top 3 publications I read for fun are…

If you want to add more, there is also…

5. What radio shows do you listen to for:

    a.   Business…

    b.   Pleasure…

6. What top three websites do you visit regularly?

Summary

- Put together a survey.
- Put together a target group to take the survey.
- Decide upon a reward for completed surveys.
- Take action on delivering it.
- Digest results, identifying the publications that your target market specifies.

Day 3 Notes

Questions I need to ask in my survey are:

1. ....

2. ....

3. ....

4. ....

5. ....

6. ....

7. ....

8. ....

9. ....

10. ....

(n.b. You don't *have* to ask this many!)

The people/groups that I will be contacting are:

My results are:

Day 4: Your Inspiration Box

Find a black box...

Or fluffy pink box file, or an empty drawer in a filing cabinet, or (god forbid) an old carrier bag... (ok, you get the idea!)

This is going to be your ideas and inspiration box and your ongoing job is to fill it with any piece of marketing or PR that comes your way and makes you think twice about the service or product it advertises. Why does it make you want to part with your money? You can include anything:

➢ Sumptuous glossy ads.
➢ A direct mail letter you get through the post.
➢ An interview in the local paper where the interviewee has cleverly managed to get their company name mentioned four times in the space of two paragraphs.
➢ Brochures or business cards that you've picked up.

Whether it's the content inside or the bold lettering that's grabbed your eye it doesn't matter. The idea is that when you're feeling uninspired about marketing and promoting your business you can go through your box and look at what has caught your eye and got you excited.

But don't keep it all to yourself.

If you start to share your treasures with others, and ask what they think, you'll find it's a great source of conversation for networking events and a valuable insight into what others find compelling and attractive.

Remember: use it for inspiration not imitation!

Summary

- Find your inspiration box and start filling it.
- Share your findings with others.
- Visit your box regularly for inspiration.

Day 5: The 100 Contact Exercise

I often see clients with world beating ideas and products that they haven't even discussed with their partners (personal, not business!), let alone friends, acquaintances, and colleagues old and new. Just think of all that untapped potential!

I know that it's often easier to talk frankly to strangers but only when you've got the confidence to stand up and shout about what you have to offer to the people who know you, whether it's your bank manager or your mother in law, will you really be able to powerfully promote it to others.

So this exercise involves you going through your address books old and new, as well as your email address folders, and putting together a list of 100 people you may not have contacted in the last few months, or even years.

Now think about something you'd like   some referrals, marketing advice, just for them to remember you perhaps. Write to them and ask for what you want. Start off with chatty non sales talk asking about them and then introduce your request. You don't have to be rude or pushy about it:

"To be honest another reason for getting in contact with you now is that I'm really trying to raise my business' profile at the moment, letting everyone know about it, and spreading the word. But, also, if you had any comments, ideas or suggestions on how to do this, then I would be really interested to hear your advice."

Do be warned, everyone loves giving advice, but don't be surprised if the response is overwhelming!

Writing something this subtle is going to be a lot less in your face and a lot more effective than saying "I've got this great new business you have to tell people about!"

Remember, you're not trying to sell directly to these people, you're simply trying to build a buzz around your promotional efforts.

If you've got a new website you could ask for their feedback. If you've got a new partner (business, not personal!) you could tell them a bit more about that person. The rule is to make it personal and chatty   not a sales pitch.

Even if you're not a start up you can still ask for help   if you're currently pushing new business for instance   and it does no harm to remind people that you are still around and available to help them too.

Just because someone isn't in business don't assume that they can't help you either. This is all about the power of networking   who knows who. Put yourself out there to see what comes right back at you.

I always suggest that this exercise is one of the first that my clients take and you'd be amazed at how many come back to me with tales of how someone's girlfriend works for the number one trade publication, or how someone's brother is the researcher for BBC's *Money Box* or whatever.

If only 5% 10% of your contacts are actually able to help you, you're still a lot better off than you were last week... and 100 more people have heard of your business or latest goals and achievements.

It's also a great exercise to really help you "own" your business and take responsibility for its future.

Summary

- Contact 100 of your friends, relatives, ex colleagues and business contacts.
- Tell them what you're up to and ask them for thoughts, ideas or support

Day 5 Notes

This week I have contacted:

1. Name: .... Contact: ....

2. Name: .... Contact: ....

3. Name: .... Contact: ....

4. Name: .... Contact: ....

5. Name: .... Contact: ....

6. Name: .... Contact: ....

7. Name: .... Contact: ....

8. Name: .... Contact: ....

9. Name: .... Contact: ....

10. Name: .... Contact: ....

11. Name: .... Contact: ....

12. Name: .... Contact: ....

13. Name: .... Contact: ....

14. Name: .... Contact: ....

15. Name: .... Contact: ....

16. Name: .... Contact: ....

17. Name: .... Contact: ....

18. Name: .... Contact: ....

19. Name: .... Contact: ....

20. Name: .... Contact: ....

21. Name: .... Contact: ....

22. Name: .... Contact: ....

23. Name: .... Contact: ....

24. Name: .... Contact: ....

25. Name: .... Contact: ....

26. Name: .... Contact: ....

27. Name: .... Contact: ....

28. Name: .... Contact: ....

29. Name: .... Contact: ....

30. Name: .... Contact: ....

31. Name: .... Contact: ....

32. Name: .... Contact: ....

33. Name: .... Contact: ....

34. Name: .... Contact: ....

35. Name: .... Contact: ....

36. Name: .... Contact: ....

37. Name: .... Contact: ....

38. Name: .... Contact: ....

39. Name: .... Contact: ....

40. Name: .... Contact: ....

41. Name: .... Contact: ....

42. Name: .... Contact: ....

43. Name: .... Contact: ....

44. Name: .... Contact: ....

45. Name: .... Contact: ....

46. Name: .... Contact: ....

47. Name: .... Contact: ....

48. Name: .... Contact: ....

49. Name: .... Contact: ....

50. Name: .... Contact: ....

51. Name: .... Contact: ....

52. Name: .... Contact: ....

53. Name: .... Contact: ....

54. Name: .... Contact: ....

55. Name: .... Contact: ....

56. Name: .... Contact: ....

57. Name: .... Contact: ....

58. Name: .... Contact: ....

59. Name: .... Contact: ....

60. Name: .... Contact: ....

61. Name: .... Contact: ....

62. Name: .... Contact: ....

63. Name: .... Contact: ....

64. Name: .... Contact: ....

65. Name: .... Contact: ....

66. Name: .... Contact: ....

67. Name: .... Contact: ....

68. Name: .... Contact: ....

69. Name: .... Contact: ....

70. Name: .... Contact: ....

71. Name: .... Contact: ....

72. Name: .... Contact: ....

73. Name: .... Contact: ....

74. Name: .... Contact: ....

75. Name: .... Contact: ....

76. Name: .... Contact: ....

77. Name: .... Contact: ....

78. Name: .... Contact: ....

79. Name: .... Contact: ....

80. Name: .... Contact: ....

81. Name: .... Contact: ....

82. Name: .... Contact: ....

83. Name: .... Contact: ....

84. Name: .... Contact: ....

85. Name: .... Contact: ....

86. Name: .... Contact: ....

87. Name: .... Contact: ....

88. Name: .... Contact: ....

89. Name: .... Contact: ....

90. Name: .... Contact: ....

91. Name: .... Contact: ....

92. Name: .... Contact: ....

93. Name: .... Contact: ....

94. Name: .... Contact: ....

95. Name: .... Contact: ....

96. Name: .... Contact: ....

97. Name: .... Contact: ....

98. Name: .... Contact: ....

99. Name: .... Contact: ....

100. Name: .... Contact: ....

Advice, feedback and follow up suggestions that resulted were:

Day 6: Discover Your Wow! Factor

You have done a fair bit of leg work so far, so this session calls for thought, rather than action.

I want you to imagine yourself in the shoes of a journalist. You're working to a deadline and your editor is hovering expectantly. You've got to find a story that will fire up both your editor and your readers. And it's got to be about *your* business.

Now, a straight forward "this is x enterprises and they do that" just won't cut it. The readers will be off and onto a different, more interesting, piece before you know it. That's if the editor doesn't throw your article in the waste bin first.

So, what is there about your business that could be of interest?

You can call this your *Wow! Factor*.

Is your business, or are you, intrinsically interesting? Were you Beyonce's stylist or the business coach for the head of a large PLC? Is your product or service so unique or astoundingly beautiful, new or valuable that journalists will want to write about it on its own merits? Are you strongly for or against something that makes you stand out?

Be strict with yourself on this one. It's easy to think that what you offer is unusual and ignore the fact that there are 15,000 other financial advisors, nutritionists, IT experts or recruitment agencies out there doing exactly the same thing.

It needs to be something special. It's that something special, that Wow! Factor, that gets your business noticed and potential clients and customers asking you to tell them more.

However, be warned. Where you trained and how qualified you are is not exciting! The main exception to that is if you have worked with a celebrity, whether it is in the mass media or in a niche market, as this does bring some reflected glory on both you and your customer. Put yourself in your customer's shoes. Imagine being able to say that your own private yoga teacher also teaches Madonna, or that your business coach's last client is on the front page of the FT today. A huge number of people are impressed by this type of "name dropping", so, if you've got names to drop, get dropping today!

If you are floundering a bit on this one then look at the publications that you have identified as your targets and take a good look at the stories that made it into their pages. What was it about the subjects that made them into a good news story?

By the end of this task I want you to come up with your *Wow! Factor*. This is going to be the crux of your press release and the core of your PR campaign.

Summary

- Decide on your WOW! Factor today.
- What's unique, interesting or newsworthy about you or your business?
- What will make people say, "Wow!"?

Day 6 Notes

Finding My Wow! Factor.

- ☐ Have I worked with a celebrity?
- ☐ Is there something unusual or interesting in my past?
- ☐ Does my company offer something unique?
- ☐ Is the background of my company of any interest – whether culturally or historically?
- ☐ Do I work in a new field that has something exciting to appeal to the press?
- ☐ What outstanding success have I had in the past?
- ☐ Do I have any particular beliefs or values that might be of interest to the outside world.
- ☐ Why am I/is my company different from everyone else?

If you are having trouble with this exercise (and it's an important exercise to get right) then it can often help to get an outsiders view on things, to give you an objective perspective. It could be an exercise that you could do jointly with a business contact.

My Wow! Factor is:

Day 7: Get Into Reading

You are now going to develop a new a new habit that will, hopefully, become part of your life forever.

Your job is to start reading a different national newspaper every day, alternating between broadsheets and tabloids. *Every* day means that weekends count too.

I also want you to read it twice. The first time you are reading it purely as a normal reader, picking out the stories that interest you as they come along.

The second time I'd like you to look at any sections (e.g. money, women's pages, health etc) that may be pertinent to your business. Plus look at other possible places that you might be able to place a story. For instance if you never read the money or business pages, familiarising yourself with them might be just the inspiration you need to start thinking about a business or financial orientated angle to get publicity for your business.

Reading newspapers on a regular basis (as opposed to just getting your news from the TV or internet) also helps you to understand the trends and preoccupations of the media world. This will help you to sound much more "on the ball" when you are being interviewed. It also works wonders for your networking skills by giving you something topical to talk about at times when you may need to break the ice or make small talk.

But don't think in terms of this week alone. I'd like you to try to adopt this habit for life. It's a wonderful way to just stop the world and spend ten or twenty minutes relaxing (but no need to feel guilty, you are still working!) with a sumptuously frothy cappuccino in your favourite local coffee house, or just putting your feet up on the sofa with a biscuit and a cup of tea. Make mine a Lapsang.

Summary

- Read a different newspaper every day   twice!

Day 7 Notes

Newspapers I've read this week...

Monday_____

Any observations on/ideas from

Tuesday_____

Any observations on/ideas from

Wednesday_____

Any observations on/ideas from

Thursday_____

Any observations on/ideas from

>

Friday_____

Any observations on/ideas from

>

Saturday_____

Any observations on/ideas from

>

Sunday_____

Any observations on/ideas from

>

Day 8: Your Press Release

Today we are going to start putting our press release together. Now, I'm not into making a huge fuss about press releases. I think they can sometimes cause more trouble than they need to.

But, if there's one thing stopping a lot of people from just getting on with their own PR, it's the idea that they can't do anything until they have a press release.

And, while I agree that having a press release is no bad thing, it is essential to stop hiding behind it and thinking of it as your one and only PR tool.

A press release is nothing more than information about you or your company that can accompany your pitch to a publication. Note that I said "accompany". Your pitch is a lot more spontaneous and fluid than a press release and, vitally, involves you, as a person and not just a motionless piece of paper.

But that said, it's still something that needs to be done so we'd better get on with it hadn't we?

My own opinion is that it is better to get something down on paper and out into the world working on our behalf than to get stressed out about the whole thing. Don't worry about creating the perfect release. If you're serious about really boosting your media profile then you'll be doing more than a few of these over time and you'll have plenty of opportunity to hone your craft.

Okay, by now, you should have decided on your *Wow! Factor*. It's what makes you special but it's not necessarily what makes you newsworthy. If you haven't decided on your Wow! Factor yet then take a look at task six.

Sometimes your Wow! Factor will make you newsworthy in its own right. Occasionally, you or your product may be just so damn interesting or sexy that you are going to take the journalist's breath away.

But more often that not you'll need something extra. You'll need a hook.

A hook is what turns your story into a news story. It's something that makes you topical. The hook is what will get the journalist to read your press release rather than just delete it. But a hook is also the reason why you are contacting that journalist *now*, and why your press release is relevant and topical *now*.

Merely announcing that your product is great and available nation wide is not a hook.

A hook can be as simple as the launch of a business, a take over bid, the publication of a book or even the fact that you and your team are running a local Marathon in chicken outfits for a local charity. Quite simply put, it is news. Take the 's' off news and you've got new! It has to be new.

Alternatively, you can turn to good old external hooks like Stop Smoking Day to promote a hypnotherapy clinic, or Valentine's Day to promote a dating Agency. You can even create your own special day or event. PR companies do this all the time. That's why we've got National Chip Week and Beautiful Smile week. All in the name of PR!

When it comes to choosing your hook your knowledge of what's new and all that is going on in your particular niche or area becomes extremely useful. If you know what's happening in the economy, housing market, celebrity and TV gossip land then you are in a much better place to spot trends and stories to use as launch pads for your own stories.

For instance, I once worked with a cosmetic dentist who sent out a fabulous release about how cosmetic dentistry can give you a face lift (without the pain and recovery period) just when the newspapers were full of speculation as to whether a prominent female actress had has surgery herself. His watchful look over the media meant that he knew when the time was right and he received marvellous coverage as a result.

Getting Down to Business

Okay, your headline needs to be clear and concise. Don't worry about puns and clever word games. Journalists really don't have time to puzzle over them – and will often change them anyway. A journalist can get over one hundred press releases a week and only have time to scan through the first few lines of the majority of them so keeping your headline simple and informative is a must.

Your first paragraph, quite simply, is your killer paragraph. It's a killer in two ways. It's a killer to write but, once written, it is the killer that will make or break your release.

All your news needs to be there. Think of the three W's. Think why, who and what. Why are you bothering to contact the journalist in the first place (i.e. what is your hook), who are you (get your name in the first paragraph not half way down the page where it might not be seen) and what – what story do you have to offer?

The best way to write your press release is to see how others have done it and take inspiration from them. To help you get started I've included some of my own releases. Take ideas from them, but don't be afraid to play around with your own ideas too. There are no set rules here but the following guidelines will help yours get picked up and used.

Summary

> • Write your press release today.

Press Release Style Sheet

✓ The press release is generally one to two sides of A4 paper.

✓ Always write for your audience. A press release targeted at women's mags like *Vogue* and *Elle* is going to be very different from one focused on magazines like *Chat* and *Bella*. Likewise a press release targeted to a golf magazine is going to be written in a completely different style to one that has been written for a motorcycle magazine. The key is to know your audience.

✓ Read the publications you're writing for to get a feel for what their readers like. If you have to write a number of versions of the same press release for different publications then so be it.

✓ Your first paragraph is the most important. It has to contain the bare bones of your story and do it in a style that grabs attention or creates curiosity.

✓ Always remember the old marketing adage of concentrating on benefits over features.

✓ Journalists are often known to lift whole sections of a press release. If your writing style already fits in with the magazine or publication's style then you have a better chance of it being used.

✓ Headlines should be short and snappy or just a quick headline to describe your release. Again, think of your audience. A clever pun or play on words will not impress the *FT*, but it might get a local newspaper or women's magazine journalist to read more.

✓ Most journalists know within a few moments of looking at the release if it's a story they will want to use. Make your information relevant and lively and, whatever you do, don't bog it down with details of how the company was set up etc. You can always provide all that on a separate sheet and offer it if the journalist shows interest in following up the story.

✓ Make sure that your contact information is correct. Your email address and telephone number should be double, even triple checked.

✓ Date your release

✓ Make it personal include quotes or testimonials from a customer/client/member of the group.

✓ Use an easy to read font like Arial or Verdana.

✗ Don't use words like "fantastic" or "great". You might think you provide a "wonderful service" but it's really up to the journalist to say so.

✗ Don't squeeze everything in instead double space and use large margins. That way journalists can scribble notes on it.

✗ Don't use technical speak even if sending it to a technical magazine. If the release really needs your thesis on Quantum Physics it can come in a separate sheet (on request).

✗ Don't send your press release as an attachment as it might never get opened. Instead cut and paste it into the body of an email (if you are emailing it).

Sample Release No. 1

Hands Off Software Training!

We all learn in different ways, which means that many people don't get the most out of traditional workshops and classes. Some will find it hard to keep to everyone else's pace and follow the structure whilst others will want to experiment on their own and not have to worry about slower learners catching up. However, *Hands Off* Training, pioneered in the States, ensures that everyone learns at their own speed, getting exactly what they need from the day and leave knowing how to apply that learning.

Software trainer Karen Roem of Karen Roem Software Training & Support (http://www.roem.co.uk) has now brought this highly successful method of training to the UK and uses it as the foundation for her *Hands Off* seminars in Microsoft office products such as Excel, Outlook, Mail Merge and others. Additionally, the *Hands Off* approach means that students' concentration, confidence and enjoyment are dramatically increased making it much more of a fulfilling experience. Traditional training can be very linear, with instructors ordering you to "click here". You learn via repetition, being shown examples to apply what you learn, but not how to apply it to you and your individual circumstances.

Hands off Training is very different. Using the concept that we can only digest 20 minutes of new material at time the intense sessions are short and focused with time in between for quizzes, games and exploration to absorb and understand what you are learning. In the past, renowned Professor and Psychologist Howard Gardner identified 8 different ways of learning   Linguistic (writing, reading, stories, puzzles), Logical Mathematical (patterns, categories, strategies and relationships), Bodily kinesthetic (dancing, crafts, sewing and woodwork), spatial (images and puzzles), musical, Interpersonal (communicating with their peers), intrapersonal (self motivated), and Naturalist (sensitivity to living things). Karen has deliberately created a training environment that covers as many of these as possible.

This approach to learning particularly helps those who may be nervous or even sent there unwillingly by their employer!

Karen's speciality is helping people really get to grips with software, showing them how it can make their job easier and their work look more polished. Seminars are deliberately jargon free and include a CD with exercises for you to practice what you learn, as well as one month post course advice personally from Karen.

Karen studied this highly effective teaching method in Kansas in 2001 where it has had excellent results. She now runs her hands off seminars alongside traditional class room training and guidance in how to get the most out of Microsoft Office Products. Clients include University of Cambridge, Cambridge Academy of English, Christian Action Housing Association, National Westminster Bank Plc, Royal Veterinary College, and University of London.

Karen is also in high demand as a *Livelink* training specialist, assisting organisations with documentation, training development and conducting hands on training classes, and has worked with Shell

International and Lloyds Register.

Dates for up and coming hands off Seminars
Excel at Excel.
Cambridge   15 September
London   29 October
Birmingham   6 December.

A jargon free look at how to untangle the mysteries of Excel and make it really work for you and your organisation.

Also coming up are:
Manage your mailshots. Whether it's the Christmas card mailout or a vital direct mail exercise, knowing how managing your Microsoft Word Mail Merge will save you precious time, money and energy.

Ditch Your Filofax. How to finally get to grips with effectively using Microsoft Outlook to create and manage both personal and business databases.

For further information:
If you would like to talk to Karen about the new *Hands Off* method, or would like to attend a seminar to see the method for yourself please speak to Karen on 01223 214177 or email her at Karen@roem.co.uk, or check out the website at www.roem.co.uk.

Ends.

Sample Release No. 2

Books For Chicks

For readers...

The new, revamped **www.chicklit.co.uk** has been launched. Full of book news, reviews, author interviews, biographies, girlie gossip, fabulous competitions and writing tips for fans of chicklit everywhere.

We've got interviews with chicklit writers like Jessica Adams. Sarah Ball, Susan Lewis, Dorothy Koomsom, (with Anna Maxted coming soon), along with Sarah Ball's diary of a writer, and reviews on chicklit novels old and new, from Freya North to Jane Green, India Knight to Lisa Jewell.

If you fancy something a bit different, we've got the best of <u>thriller chicks</u> and <u>literary chicks</u> to tempt you...as well as look at the offerings from the boys in <u>Lad Lit</u>.

You can buy any book or DVD featured on www.chicklit.co.uk through <u>www.Amazon.co.uk</u>. Just click on the link or image and you'll be taken through to the Amazon site where you can order your product (and browse around for more) and buy online through their safe and efficient ordering facility.

For writers...

And if you're inspired to try and write your own novel, we've got tons of help and advice on writing a book, getting and staying motivated, finding your plot, finding an agent and eventually getting published   all from experienced and published authors like Susan Lewis, Susannah Bates and Jessica Adams.

You can find a writing buddy on our <u>forum</u>, or just chat with other readers about your favourite (or least favourite) author, the latest book releases, your lives, relationships and ideas.

And each month we're offering free wine to the best book reviewer!

For further information contact Paula on 07941 244343, or **<u>mail@chicklit.co.uk</u>** / **<u>www.chicklit.co.uk</u>**

ends

Sample Release No. 3

Beverley Knowles Fine Art
Opens New London Gallery

Fine Art finder and online art dealer Beverley Knowles (www.beverleyknowles.com), specialist in women's art, is pleased to announce the acquisition and opening of the Beverley Knowles gallery at Bedales at London's Borough Market, SE1

A graduate of Goldsmiths, after 5 years with respected Bond Street art dealer Anthony Mould Ltd, Beverly launched Beverley Knowles Fine Art in 2002 and became one of the few art dealers (possibly even the only in the London) that devote themselves entirely to the arena of women's art. Academically, it's an area that has attracted a huge amount of research and research but, until now, the same amount of interest has not been forthcoming in the commercial arena.

Beverly shows the best of female art as she's sees it, mixing established artists like Bridget Reilly, Sandra Blow, Elisabeth Frink, with talented new comers like Sydna Younson, Carol Fulton, Karen Stamper, Martha Hussey and Shelley Theodore.

Known for providing a service that is out of the ordinary, Beverley offers clients the opportunity to live with their chosen pieces for a week in their own homes before finally purchasing them. She is happy to visit clients with a selection of work she feels may be to their taste, and in doing so, finds that she creates a strong understanding of her client's needs and preferences.

She Exists
"Of course there's no such thing as a totally objective person, except Almighty God, if she exists".
 Historian Antonia Fraser.

Opening 10th February, the exhibition She Exists will contain works of art (and furniture!) from the following four artists:

Klari Reis
Klari Reis produces beautiful richly coloured abstract paintings using an unusual medium called epoxy polymer, a synthetic plastic derived from crude oil that is more commonly used to water seal boats. This intriguing plastic she pours over the aluminium base that she uses as a canvas to create a highly plasticized and satisfyingly touchable smooth colourful surface.

Although it is not immediately apparent, her subject matter is the complex workings of the internal body examined on a microscopic scale. Each one of her compositions shows an image of the molecular appearance of different medicinal drugs as seen through a microscope. Reis is fascinated by bioengineering and her work aims to interpret the body's responses to biological technology through examining and creating her own ideas about the functions, colours, shapes and sizes of what is going on beneath the surface of the skin.

The finished works are super modern and very tactile polished pieces that look particularly good in a contemporary loft apartment.

You can see some of Klari's work at:
http://www.beverleyknowles.com/artists/page.php?artist_id=36

Claire Pettinati
Claire Francesca Pettinati takes infamous London landmarks as her subject matter (the Palace of Westminster, the Millennium Wheel and the Tower of London to name a few) and interprets them with a refreshingly modern twist through the eyes of a young contemporary Londoner. She worked as a freelance illustrator for five years producing weekly drawings of London for the Observer newspaper, before turning her love of London into a fine art. She is hugely inspired by London its culture, atmosphere, energy and its architecture. Only in London, she believes, could architectural giants as diverse as Christopher Wren's St Paul's Cathedral lie comfortably alongside Norman Foster's Erotic Gherkin.

Margarite Horner

Margarite paints huge contemplative monochrome landscapes that transport us to the rugged, powerful land and time of Heathcliffe. Dark and brooding yet delicate and romantic, these pictures are a must for anybody with a love of the great outdoors!

Nicole Fulton

Nicole restores and re upholsters period antique furniture using contemporary fabrics and designs to bring the old into the new. Each chair, chaise longe and sofa becomes a one off piece – alternative, elegant and contemporary.

Beverley has chosen this eclectic mix to show modern art and antiques side by side, as happens in people's homes   art for beauty's sake, rather than because it fits a particular period or trend.

Beverley Knowles Fine Art at Bedale Gallery, 4 Bedale Street, Borough Market, London, SE1 9AL, Tel: 020 7378 7732. Opening Hours are Thursday 11am – 7pm, Friday 11am – 7pm and Saturday 11am – 7pm.

For further information, or to interview Beverly or any of the artists please contact Beverley on xxxxx

Day 8 Notes

My headline is:

My hook is (your first paragraph – your news):

My Wow! Factor is (the main body of your release):

More details on my/the story are:

Brief company or personal history is:

My contact details are:

Day 9: Get A Buddy

Having a PR buddy might sound a bit naff but this type of relationship can be invaluable. The idea is that you read each others press releases, swap contacts and ideas and provide both support and a frank appraisal of each others work.

Choosing the right buddy is vital. You need to find someone in a field that's not too dissimilar from your own – and it's great if they have a similar target market. But at the same time you don't want to choose a direct competitor as your buddy. A company running corporate fun days doing activities like paint balling or trike racing could buddy up with someone who wants to supply the corporate world with personal concierge services to ease the life of employees, or a wine tasting events company. In this case you share the same market, but you aren't competing with each other.

You also need someone who:

> ➢ Will take PR as seriously as you.
> ➢ Has enough time to give you and your work the attention it needs.
> ➢ Is not afraid to say "sorry but this is just plain boring/badly written/absolute rubbish!"
> ➢ Wants to raise their own business profile and would see this as a win/win situation.
> ➢ Isn't precious and can take criticism.
> ➢ You trust to give you honest feedback.

Think about the business contacts you know. Who could be your buddy?

Don't be put off if the first person you approach doesn't seem overwhelmed with gratitude for the idea. It may take a while before you come up with the perfect person but you will, eventually.

And, as soon as you do find that special person, get that press release over to them for their thoughts and opinions.

Summary

- Choose and approach a possible PR buddy today.
- Send them your press release to critique.

Day 9 Notes

A shortlist of people who I can approach to be my PR buddy...

Day 10: Become Radio Savvy

Now that you've started reading newspapers on a regular basis I'm going to suggest that you start listening to the radio as you get dressed in the morning, as you work (if that's possible), as you drive home from work and as you peel the spuds in the evening.

Quite honestly, *Radio 4* is the best starting place for anyone who wants to become aware of all the opportunities out there (think *Money Box* and *Woman's Hour* just for starters) but there are also many local and regional stations that have regular talk shows that could be perfect for you.

As well as keeping up with gossip, news, names and who's who in the media, you are also actively listening for opportunities that may be waiting for you such as talk slots for members of the community, expert phone ins and topical comments interspersed with news stories.

Try to listen to something new every day. You never know, you just might find a hidden gem and become a regular listener.

Summary

- **To listen to at least one different radio show every day.**

Day 10 Notes

Radio Shows that I have listened to this week are...

Monday_____

Content_____

Possibilities for PR

```
[                                                        ]
[                                                        ]
[                                                        ]
[                                                        ]
```

Tuesday_____

Content_____

Possibilities for PR

```
[                                                        ]
[                                                        ]
[                                                        ]
[                                                        ]
```

Wednesday_____

Content_____

Possibilities for PR

```
[                                                        ]
[                                                        ]
[                                                        ]
[                                                        ]
```

Thursday_____

Content_____

Possibilities for PR

```
┌─────────────────────────────────────────────────────────┐
│                                                         │
│                                                         │
│                                                         │
│                                                         │
└─────────────────────────────────────────────────────────┘
```

Friday_____

Content_____

Possibilities for PR

```
┌─────────────────────────────────────────────────────────┐
│                                                         │
│                                                         │
│                                                         │
│                                                         │
└─────────────────────────────────────────────────────────┘
```

Saturday_____

Content_____

Possibilities for PR

```
┌─────────────────────────────────────────────────────────┐
│                                                         │
│                                                         │
│                                                         │
│                                                         │
└─────────────────────────────────────────────────────────┘
```

Sunday_____

Content_____

Possibilities for PR

Day 11: Start Connecting

So, you've written your press release, and found someone who will critique it objectively for you. You've also become acquainted with the publications and radio shows that will help you to increase and grow your business. Now you are going to start approaching journalists, building up a contact list, and getting some idea of the process involved in submitting PR material.

Now you're really going to start making new friends and contacts.

And make those friends count. Now that you've conducted your media research you'll have a canny idea of what magazines and newspapers your prospective clients and customers read and what radio programmes they listen to. We're now going to take the next step and make contact with your chosen show or publication.

The best way to do this, rather than go in with all guns blazing, is to choose one publication at a time and approach the editorial assistant, editor's PA or researcher for radio, and merely ask for some of their time for a quick chat about the publication or programme. Who is the best person to approach and how do they like to be approached? Is it by email, post or telephone? Is it worth visiting their publication in person with a sample of your goods? Ask them for help, but as a business person not a PR person. Keep the conversation light and flowing and be generous with thanking them for helping you. Make sure you learn their name and what they do and send them a follow up email or even a little card thanking them. You never know, in two years time they could be the editor!

Ten minutes chatting to someone in this way can pay dividends – it also earns you an insider contact on the magazine. Keep them informed of what you are doing and if you hold any events make sure they also get an invite too. Make them one of your key contacts and keep them happy.

Once you have all the names of your contacts get your press release off to them in the required format (email or letter). At the moment we are looking at this more as a good kick start to get your name out there and noticed by the people that need to know. Think of it as the first step in building your relationship with the press.

Summary

- Choose your publications.
- Spend some time on the telephone making contacts and notes.

Day 11 Notes

Publication...	Person I Spoke To...	Recommendations...

Day 12: Become An Expert

Now you are going to start on the road to becoming an expert.

Have you ever noticed how the same people's names always seem to appear in magazines and newspaper articles that quote them as a source of information and advice on their own particular subject, whether it is life coaching or investment banking?

Well, they don't just get there by accident. They, or their PR Company, have generally put in a pretty concerted effort to get them known as an expert in their field. And here's how you can become one too…

Be a specialist and define your niche. Don't just choose the whole of your industry; choose a particular part that has relevance for people's lives (or their money!). For instance if you are a life coach choosing a particular area of coaching (say finding a new job) is going to be more successful than trying to set yourself up as an expert on the industry as a whole. Likewise if you deal with investing people's money, talking about investing for your children's education and further education will bring you better results as specialist situations will bring you into the mind of the journalists.

You might have to tweak your press release and produce a version that concentrates on this particular niche. But now you have your master release you should be able to play around with it without too much angst and tears.

Put together some tips, say a "top 10 list", on your niche. Make them practical and informative nuggets of valuable information.

Decide how often you are going to send your tips out – weekly, monthly, fortnightly? Sit down and make sure that you have enough to last you a good few months. Do you need to come up with any more?

Send that press release out, together with your tip of the month/week on investments, caring for your teeth/getting new clients.

Make a date in your diary to send a new "tips article" one out every month/week/fortnight. Don't forget to include your press release at the same time.

Make a date in your diary to remind yourself to spend some time coming up with new tips.

When someone takes up one of your tips and publishes it, put it together in a portfolio that you can build up and use to enhance your reputation as an expert.

On future press and marketing info you can now say as featured in *Accountancy Magazine* or whatever. Do remember, however, that you need to get their permission before you can reproduce the feature.

Experts have to be adept at putting difficult ideas and concepts into layman's language, and often the most successful experts have a call to action that anyone can handle. So keep your tips practical and easy to read – try them out on a willing friend or your PR buddy first.

Summary

- Decide on your expert niche.
- Put together a list of tips that will last you a few months.
- Send your first tip out, accompanied by your press release.

Day 12 Notes

I am an expert on:

My tips for the next 2 months are:

Publications that I will send these to are:

Day 13: Community Service

Let's get your business recognised by the local community.

Now, like many of you, I do a fair bit of networking. Both online and in the flesh. I've been contacted by some fascinating people that I would normally never have come across in my daily life, and met some lovely people that often turn out to be more than just business contacts.

But don't forget that sometimes one of the biggest and most simple networking steps you can take is becoming part of your local community.

This can mean anything from becoming a school governor, to taking on the role of treasurer in your own Residents Association to coaching a women's' football team. From a publicity angle you are getting your name out there amongst local people who may well be keener to help you and forge links than someone you've merely chatted to online. School, community and local charity events often get reported by the local press, which all helps your name to become recognised in the local area.

And, of course, you'll really be helping to make a difference; something which may be much more appealing than standing around with a lukewarm glass of wine and trying to avoid being sold something you don't want by the person standing next to you.

Of course, only do this is if it appeals. There's no point in forcing yourself to do any form of networking if it's not in your comfort zone. You'll never keep it up (one reason I just don't do breakfast events!).

So, consider this:

➤ You must be genuinely interested in what you are doing. There's got to be some passion there as it can and will get pretty tedious at times.

➤ Realise that this is a long term promotion strategy.

➤ Make sure you can give the time and energy that the position needs. You will do more harm than good (to both yourself and the organisation) if you have to back out later because you're spreading yourself too thinly.

➤ Try and tailor your contribution to your skills. If you are an accountant, offer to become treasurer. If you're a graphic designer, design the brochures; if you're a PR or events organiser, do the PR or organisation for an event.

Spend some time researching and thinking about what is going on in your local area that you can become involved in. And, take action on it. Phone the organiser, make the meeting, drop them an email and offer your help.

Summary

- Investigate and decide how you are going to become involved in your local community.
- Take action on it.

Day 13 Notes

Local/community possibilities are:

Those that appeal are:

Those that fit in time wise with me are:

Actions to take:

Day 14: Make Friends

Now you are going to make a huge step and befriend a journalist.

If you've got designs on publicity you need to know journalists. And when I say, "know them", I mean that when you pick up the telephone and speak to them you won't have to explain who you are all over again.

But, I'm going to suggest that you take your relationship forward another step and *adopt* a journalist. What you're after is a semi formal relationship with a reporter, writer, journalist or editor who has the media training, knows how newspapers and magazines work, and can advise you in your campaign.

It doesn't matter if it's someone on a publication you have little interest in, or your best friend's sister who just happens to hold an editorial position at the *Guardian*. What I'd like you to look for is someone who's happy for you to run your article ideas or press release past them. You want to find someone who's happy and willing to give any suggestions for improvements or more effective angles. It's their skill you're after, not their position or contacts.

And, just to make sure that they prove a reliable source of help, you're going to offer them something in return. This could be a retainer, free samples of your own goods or services, or you could barter an arrangement where you help them in some other way. But, having someone with editorial knowledge on board to help you in your own publicity manoeuvres is a wonderful resource.

Who do you know who might help?

Summary

- Find and adopt a pet journalist.

Day 14 Notes

Journalists or Writers that I know and can approach are:

Day 15: Personality Centred PR

Whether you're publicising an event that has a strong lead character involved, or your own company, you are probably wondering about personal PR. This means using a person as a hook for your campaign – using your background and life story and the reasons why you started your company providing holidays to Iceland can be a lot more press friendly than a dry press release about trips to Iceland that your company offers.

The press like people and the stories around them. Personalities are interesting. As such, you'll find it's much easier to get into publications and on the radio with a people or person lead story than it is with a product lead story.

Quite often, business, trade and professional publications have a regular profile spot where they report on a "person of the month" or similar and having something more exciting to offer than, "I like reading, golf and poker" will often be the thing that swings your place in that spot. Oh yes, and having a good photo. It doesn't have to show you as a Brad Pitt or Jennifer Anniston; just someone approachable, happy, and with a sparkle in their eye!

The pros

✓ It is easier to get journalists interested.

✓ Your potential customers can form a bond with you. This really comes into play when you are providing an extremely personal service such as coaching – so that when they do consider using a coaching service, they will (hopefully!) come to you.

✓ It can fulfil a common desire to become famous as well as rich!

The Cons

✗ You're setting yourself up for skeletons to come bounding out of the closet.

✗ It's also quite a subjective process. Using a personality to sell something means that some people are not going to like your personality and therefore won't consider what you've got to sell, even though it might actually be perfect for them.

✗ The press can be harsh. A journalist can decide they don't like you for no other reason than personal dynamics and that can be reflected in their piece.

✗ You've got to be confident and flexible enough to carry the campaign for your product. Are you happy to give radio interviews or talk on the spur of the moment to journalists? Are you flexible enough to drop everything when they phone and want a quote on your industry there and then – even if you're just rushing off to make an important meeting or pick the kids up from school?

✗ If your chosen field is technical or fast moving, you've got to be on the ball and up to date. Let the knowledge slip and you could be heading for a fall!

So, how do you do it?

You'll need to think about what makes you and your life interesting. It might be a good idea to get friends, family and colleagues on board to help out with their ideas too. Is your background of interest? Were you a pole dancer before becoming an internet entrepreneur? ... (and if you were, would you rather keep quiet about it?). Are you a single mother, juggling running a business with bringing up four children under five? Is it the sheer force of your personality that makes you interesting? Do you have strong views on a particular subject? Are you passionate about something bigger than just your business?

Putting together a press release about yourself takes skill. You have to try to look at yourself from the outside – what would a journalist and a reader find interesting about you?

Take a look at the sort of publications that you'd like to appear in – what kind of stories do they use? Angle your press release so that you too fit into the type of stories that they run.

Finally, you'll need good photos and unless you have a very talented amateur friend, get them done professionally, but avoid the standard head and shoulders business portrait. Find a photographer who has that something extra. If you want something unusual, using natural light in the outdoors then I can recommend Sue Kennedy of www.blueeyesphoto.com. But you can also search for a portrait photographer on www.bipp.com.

Summary

- Consider what there is about you personally that would make a good story for your target publications.
- Put together a press release and photographs for this.
- Send your personal story out to the relevant journalists.

Day 15 Notes

A list of things about me that the press might find interesting:

My target publications/shows that publish personal stories or profiles:

Day 16: Make Links – Get Links

The more relevant links there are to your site, the more likely it is that people will actually be able to find you through relevant browsing. Forget web rings, and reciprocal links with just any old bod who contacts you out of the blue (I was recently contacted by a company making sash windows. Why on earth they thought www.doyourownpr.com visitors might be their customers I have no idea). Instead, make your link swapping a highly focused and strategic campaign.

If you don't already have one, set aside a page on your website for links to other sites (you can call it "resources", "links" or even "other places of interest"). Yes, there is the possibility that you will be leading people away from your own site, but if you choose well with a selection of sites that will be of some use to your visitors, then you will be providing a useful service and might well provoke them to bookmark your site (you can even add a helpful note on your page to remind them to do this).

Consider your target market. What sort of sites might lead them to yours? What would be a logical step from your site and vice versa? For instance a site selling beauty products made from entirely natural ingredients might consider linking to children's sites (anxious parents wanting additive free products), women's sites, general beauty sites, career woman sites, green and ecology orientated sites. Yes, of course, you can spread your links further afield, but why waste your precious time on sites that are unlikely to send you the customers *you* want.

At the same time, consider your vistors. Who might they want to read about and visit?

Set yourself a target for the week. It could be 20, 50 or even 100 reciprocal links if you want to really go for it, but have a number in mind and enjoy the feeling of satisfaction as you climb steadily towards your target.

Compose your link swapping suggestion email. Something simple and short is best, perhaps along the lines of

"I recently came across your site xxxxx, and enjoyed reading it. I think it would be particularly relevant to the visitors of xxxxx (your site) and wondered if you would be interested in exchanging links. I would be very happy to put you on my links/resources section (you do have one by now don't you?) and as soon as I hear from you I can put you on the list to go up."

Then just wait for your replies – don't hassle. When someone says yes, respond with a link and then, a few weeks later, check their site. If you can't see your own link there a polite reminder is fine and should do the trick.

Summary

- Embark on an intensive link swapping campaign.
- Set yourself a target number and carry on until you have reached that goal.

Day 16 Notes

Sites I have contacted...

Day 17: Organise A Behind the scenes Visit

Now, if you are stuck behind a desk all day this task might not be that helpful, so I apologise in advance. But if you work in a location or area of work that is either very photogenic, or just downright unusual, then you could consider throwing your doors open to the press.

Some ideas that you might like to follow up could be:

- ❑ Approaching journalists to do a behind the scenes "day in the life of" piece.
- ❑ Challenging journalists to take your place and become a jewellery maker, sommelier or pig farmer for the day (hints of the Generation Game perhaps?)
- ❑ Offering a competition prize of a day behind the scenes (with on the job training) at your establishment. Great if you own a funky bar and are offering a day learning to mix cocktails for instance, with all the relevant press coverage of course.

So, have a little think. Is there anything that you do, or anywhere that you go (flower market? Racing circuit? Trading floor?) that you can turn into a hook and entice the press to come and visit you?

Send them a covering note or email along with your press release asking them to come and visit or offering a visit as an applicable prize to their audience.

Summary

- Consider what you can offer for a press visit.
- Take action and invite the relevant press.

Day 17 Notes

What I have, what I do or where I am that may be unusual enough to persuade the press to visit me:

Day 18: Learn From Your Competitors

Why beat down that virgin pathway when you can learn from the success (and mistakes) of others? You could save yourself a great deal of time and energy (and maybe even money) just by looking at what somebody else's business does.

So, how do you go about it?

Ascertain exactly who your main competitors are. How do they rank against you in coverage, size and success?

Where have you seen them in the media over the last 6 12 months? If it was a feature, did they come across well? Analyse what you have seen and be objective. As an independent customer would you be swayed into parting your cash?

What is their unique selling point or *Wow! Factor?* What, in your opinion, is it about them that made the editor or journalist use them for a story?

How do you compare? Do you offer a better, cheaper or more interesting service, or do you operate on a very different USP perhaps? They may present a clinical faceless (but efficient) front to the world, and this may suit them well. But perhaps you can get leverage from a different front – perhaps exploiting your warmth, experience and friendliness by concentrating on personal PR.

If you're interested in expanding the process online you can check out your competitor and who is linking to them by visiting www.alltheweb.com and typing in your competitors URL. Any sites linking to them should be displayed (but don't forget they can do the same for you!) This might give you some ideas and inspiration… as well as letting you know what you're up against.

Summary

- List your competitors
- How are you different from them?
- How can you show your potential customers that your differences are valuable?

Day 18 Notes

My competitors are:

Their Wow! Factor is:

I have seen them featured in these publications:

Websites linking to them (that I might also be able approach) are:

I am different from them in these ways:

Day 19: Spread Your Net A Little Wider

At the moment you're probably limiting your PR to the publications that you've seen on the newsagents' shelf, or those that you've come across as a result of your work or business.

For this task I'd like you to go back to the media guide that I asked you to get right at the beginning of this workbook. The two that I mentioned were *Hollis* and the *Writers and Artists Yearbook* and, if you've done your homework, you'll have at least one of those sitting on your dedicated PR shelf right now.

What I'd like you to do over the course of this week is to read that book from cover to cover (yes, you can skim read) looking out for new publications that might be applicable to your needs. These could be your target clients' trade publications or professional press, which would be why you perhaps weren't familiar with the names. It could be a niche publication, or something that is just so "on the edge" that it's perfect for an unusual campaign.

If you can't get hold of these titles immediately, a good ruse (but remember, you didn't get it from me) is to phone up the advertising department and ask for a media pack and copy of the magazine as you may consider advertising in it but want to check it out to make sure it's right for you. This is not a lie, I hasten to add because if it is 100% perfect for you I expect that some day you might consider advertising in it. A hot advertising sales department will get a copy off to you that day. Just make sure that you don't give in to the sales phone calls that will undoubtedly follow.

Summary

> • Go through your media guide and look for new opportunities.

Day 19 Notes

New publications for me to look at are:

Day 20: Role Modelling

After taking a look at your competitors you can now learn from those you admire.

Modelling yourself or your business on those that have already achieved success is a tried and tested idea. And you don't have to carbon copy one individual or company. You can choose bits and pieces from whoever has inspired you with their ability to publicise their business.

1. Who do you admire? Don't just think of people and companies within your own industry, but cross trades and industries. How do they rank against you in profile and success? Can you see yourself in their shoes in the future? As I was a teenager in the eighties, I find that a lot of my role models date from those that I first became aware of at that time – Richard Branson, Anita Roddick, Lynne Franks, and Vivienne Westwood. Recent inspirations have included Fiona Harrold, Coffee Republic's Sahar Hashemi, writer JK Rowling and chefs Nigella Lawson and Jamie Oliver. But you don't have to just look to household business names. I also take note of what perhaps lesser known, but equally well respected people like wealth coach Nicola Cairncross and coach Chris Barrow are doing and learn from them.

2. Remember modelling doesn't mean copying. It means taking parts of what they do and applying them to your own business, in your own unique way.

3. Where have you seen them in the media over the last 6 12 months? If it was a feature, did they come across well? Analyse what you have seen – as an independent customer would you be swayed into parting with your cash?

4. What is their unique selling point or *Wow! Factor?*

7. What, in your opinion, is it about them that made the editor or journalist use them for a story? Does this inspire any ideas for your own Wow! Factor?

5. How do they deal with the media – is it graciously, with respect? Do they manipulate and court the media with stunts like balloon flights over far flung destinations or do they do what they have to do, regardless of what the media says? Can you learn anything from their media style?

Summary

- Decide who you admire.
- Ascertain what you can learn from them.

Day 20 Notes

Businesses and People I admire (and why) are:

Their *Wow! Factor* is:

Aspects of their business or PR can I model without copying are:

Day 21: Get On The Radio

Now that you're an expert, with an easily identifiable niche and lots of helpful information to impart to the general public pitch yourself to a radio talk show.

Many radio shows today are more than happy for you to speak to them on the telephone, so you can make yourself comfortable on the sofa with a cup of tea while you wait for your moment of glory. I have one client who regularly makes outside broadcasts from his mobile phone just outside the British Library.

So, how do you get on the radio?

Start by making friends with the receptionist at your chosen radio station, and ask them about the various talk programmes on air and run your ideas by him or her. Usually, they will be able to point you in the right direction and give you a number of researchers or producers from different shows who might be interested in considering you as a guest. Ask to speak to them or leave a message on their voicemail. Make email a last resort as you want the person to person contact that allows them to hear your enthusiasm and makes them think, "He'd make a good guest."

Once you've got through to them you can give them a good verbal indication of how marvellous a guest you would be. If they are interested they will either say so on the spot or ask you to send over your press release so they can think about it.

If you've been on the radio before and have a tape of the appearance offer to send it in.

When you get a, "yes please", don't stop there. Carry on with the rest of your prospects and become a radio star!

Summary

- Approach radio shows and offer yourself as a guest.

Day 21 Notes

Radio Shows that I have contacted are:

Day 22: Read Some Letters

Your task this week is to look at the letters pages of your target magazines.

If you're a regular reader of a particular publication, whether it's *The Times*, *Media Week*, *Button's Weekly* or *Men's Health* magazine, you've probably cast your eye over the letters to the editor. Some of these fall into the "you're such a great publication" category, while others actively comment on an issue of the day, or a recently published article or news item.

I'd like you to spend some time sussing out some publications that you'd like to include in this exercise. They can be your own trade or professional publications or a broad consumer title, or a mixture of both.

Spend some time looking at the sort of letters that are published. Are the publications looking for letters that are controversial, or do they tend to publish congratulatory letters in the, "You're such a great magazine" vein? Are the letters commenting on articles that have appeared in past issues or are they topical and reflect what's going on in the news or that particular industry?

Summary

- Investigate the letters pages of your target publications.

Day 22 Notes

Name of Publication	Type of letter published

I have decided to approach these publications:

Day 23: Hold Competitions

If you're keen on getting more traffic coming through to your website then posting competitions will help push up the numbers. You can offer your own goods or services as a competition prize, or get together with someone else and promote their product or service. They get free publicity; you get goodies to give away.

Once your competition is online, make the most of it by posting it on www.loquax.co.uk. Within a day or two of competitions being listed, most sites will see traffic increase significantly. Yes, some of that traffic is only coming to look because of the prizes, but out of that a proportion may be your possible market group, and it will certainly help in the bid to raise your profile.

Summary

- Post a competition on your website.
- Tell people about it on loquax.co.uk

Day 23 Notes

Competition Prizes will be:

The closing date for the competition will be:

The text for the competition will be:

Any follow up actions? (e.g. source image to accompany the competition and use on the site)

Day 24: Offer Competition Prizes

Use competitions in other publications to achieve publicity.

Choose one or more of your target titles that run reader competitions or offers and ask them if they'd like to offer your goods or services as a prize. You'll need to do some investigating to find out the right person to speak to (just ask who organises the competitions   many titles have a designated person). This is definitely a telephone rather than email task.

Once they've agreed in principal you can negotiate how many/much you'd be prepared to give away, the retail cost of that, plus what you'd like in exchange (e.g. link, photo, text, contact details, or whatever).

Do be aware that many magazines have a minimum prize limit, so that each winner must receive, for instance, a prize of at least £50 in value.

Make sure this is put in writing, even if you have to do it yourself, for your own piece of mind.

Summary

- Approach other publications, businesses and organisations with competition prizes.

Day 24 Notes

Competition prizes I am prepared to give away are:

Titles/Publications/Shows/Organisations I have approached are:

People willing to run competitions are (specify names and dates):

Day 25: Hold A Talent Contest

Still on the theme of competitions, your task is to organise a contest.

I recently did some work with a client who had run a local contest amongst design students in the three colleges that run design courses in her locality. The brief was to come up with a design for packaging that would be used on a national basis. A number of local papers and radio stations covered the contest, as well as the student media, and the results were that she got a beautifully designed product, lots of free publicity (with great photos of herself and the packaging), plus her company name became part of the local community.

The winner had the kudos of having their design taken up by a national company, as well as a small monetary award. What a brilliant win win situation.

Your task this week is to see if you can use this idea to help your business.

So, let's break this down into manageable chunks.

What is your equivalent of a design contest? In fact, you may even want to run a design contest. If I were to run this I might approach any of the local Universities (and there are a fair few of them) that run Media courses in London and organise a competition to find the PR prodigy of the year! I'd ask them to come up with a PR strategy for a fictitious client.

I would then put together the rules and regulations for entrance and contact the appropriate colleges (it's important to get their support) before approaching the press with a press release outlining the contest.

I would gather together a board of judges – not just myself – people from the local community, tutors from media courses, and maybe a local businessperson who has run their own successful PR campaign.

I would have an independent person administrating the entries so that both myself and the judges can remain independent.

After picking the winner I would announce this to the press and arrange a time for the prize giving. Prizes could be anything from hard cash, to a work experience place, to a job offer, to a slap up meal for two… believe me the press coverage and public image would be worth it.

This task involves a lot of organisation but it is certainly worth the effort, and not just for the publicity. You may well find the perfect employee, or someone that you'd like to work with in the future. And having someone else bring fresh ideas, enthusiasm and perhaps a new look at your own business from an objective outsider's point of view is always an interesting and valuable exercise.

Summary

> - Organise a contest to gain publicity and new input into your business.

Day 25 Notes

Ideas for a Contest:

The Prize I will offer:

Institutions to approach (if any):

Publications to approach:

Day 26: Write A Letter

Remember those letters to the editor I asked you to study for a recent task? Well, now we are going to do something about it.

Letters to the Editor are yet another possible way that you can get the name of your business in front of people's eyes and the beauty of it is that it's free (apart from buying a few copies of the publication for research). You can even choose to be controversial to make sure people really remember who you are. So, what's the best way to go about it?

Choose your publication. What are your prospective customers likely to read? What titles did you come up with from your previous research?

Study the letters – are they comments on past stories, controversial postings about news today, or hints and tips for the reader?

As you get used to the style and content on things the publication prints, you'll find something that inspires or motivates you to write your own letter. Remember to mention your business in some subtle way (how does this issue impact on you and your company?) and make sure that your name and contact details are supplied with the letter.

You may have to write more than once to get published, and you should try more than one publication (but not with the same letter obviously!).

Consider this a small but significant part of your overall campaign to get your business noticed. Most columns accept email comments so it is something that you can do with minimal effort and outlay.

Read the letters column of every publication you come across on a regular basis and work out how you can make them into an opportunity for you. It is also extremely valuable in working towards your previous goal of becoming an expert.

Summary

- Write at least one letter to the editor.

Day 26 Notes

Name of publication	Summary of letter	Date sent/published

Day 27: Make The News

This session is all about becoming a news item. Which means that you need to think about what that means in terms of news for your industry. Is a piece in the consumer newspapers or local or regional daily going to be of use to you, or will something in your trade paper's news section be more relevant?

Often the simplest way to become a news item is to use some statistics and play around with them, to tell your story. These can be from a national study that has just been published that relates to a problem your business can solve.

Alternatively, you can get your own facts and figures together, even if it means standing around in a cold and wet shopping centre for a couple of hours with a pen, clipboard and nice smile. So:

- ❑ Get your facts and figures to work up a story.
- ❑ Put your story together and either send it out with your press release, or use it to create a brand new press release.
- ❑ Get it out to the news editors.

When you are planning a news campaign it's worth taking five minutes at the beginning to find out exactly when press day is and when the deadlines for each issue will be. If it's a weekly, there will be a cut off day for that issue of the publication, and you'll also know that after this time it's not a good idea to phone as everyone will be very busy.

Monthlies won't be so hectic but again there will be deadline dates and times when the staff are busy, "putting it to bed". Finding out these little details also means that you can find out their quiet time, the best time for you to get hold of somebody. You don't have to speak to an editor to find out this sort of information. The receptionist or an editorial assistant will be able to help you just as well, and just might be able to give you some extra insider knowledge.

Summary

- Use a survey to put together a news story.

Day 27 Notes

The survey I have used concludes:

Newspapers and publications I have approached are:

Day 28: Hot Dates

Now you are going to make some hot dates!

How often are you contacting the press? Whenever you have a piece of news? With a twice yearly press campaign? For any chance of long term successful PR you have to woo the press with persistent courting. You need to remind them regularly that you are available, willing and ready for anything.

So, as well as your customary press releases, it also makes sense to tickle the press with regular titbits. It may take six months for them to take effect, but it's a low cost medium effort tactic that can really pay dividends in the long term.

You've made a start, but how do you go about keeping up the momentum long term?

Get out your diary or go and buy a wall calendar.

Mark off a regular day each month – say the 1st Monday of every month.

These hot dates should be designated as Press Days. Keep them sacred. Make sure that no other meetings or long lunches (unless they are with a journalist!) get slipped in. These days should be totally given over both practically and mentally to your long term PR tickler campaign.

Decide how you are going to contact the press. It could be in the form of your expert tip of the month, a news item written on a monthly basis and tailored to the events of the moment, or you could cheat a little and send them your monthly newsletter.

Now set aside a day to revisit your press mailing list. This should have come a long way since you started. You have made new contacts and scribbled out old ones that have moved on. Make a note of who you now feel is worth contacting. Would they prefer to be contacted by mail or email? Don't forget radio and the web.

You can also use these dates to post new content on your own website.

Summary

- Make some hot dates – press dates.

Day 28 Notes

Dates I have noted on my calendar or diary are:

Day 29: Write An Article

In this session you are going to write an article. Forget any worries about being a bad writer, you can always ask, pay or beg someone to polish or re write the article for you. Your aim today is to get some thoughts and information down on paper and in a form that will be valuable for someone else.

The first step is to decide what type of publication you are going to write for. Personally and professionally I always prefer the internet. Articles are shorter (around 450 words) because people don't want to read pages and pages of text, you can use headlines and bullet points to liven things up and in terms of marketing. And the beauty of it is that people don't have to remember your name or your website as they can just click through to your site from the article. Simple but effective.

If you've got somewhere in particular in mind then do take a look at the website before you start writing.

Otherwise just find somewhere quiet and conducive and start writing. Aim to finish the thing today, at least the first draft. Then put it away for a few days and let it mull over in your head. When you come back to it you'll be refreshed and invigorated and should be able to edit and tidy it very easily.

All you then have to do is offer it as free content (in exchange for a link) to a website. If you've got a newsletter and you're eager for new subscribers then make sure you mention your free newsletter in your intro or biography. Also keep the copyright by inserting the following statement (obviously using your name) into the text... *Copyright © Paula Gardner 2004. All rights reserved.*

This means that you can offer it to other websites and even post it on your own. A double whammy!

Once you've proved to yourself you can do this it will be easier to come up with a number of additional topics to write on.

When you've reached this point you can start to think about approaching an editor (website or otherwise) about the possibility of you writing a column. Put together a good proposal with a list of columns (you'll probably need at least 4 6 to show that you can come up with high quality ideas), a biography explaining why you would be a good person for the job, examples of your past articles and a sample column. In some cases you may even be able to negotiate regular payment for your words. Just think – you'd be getting paid to promote yourself. It's a PR dream come true!

Summary

- Write an article today.

Day 29 Notes

Website I would like to writes article for:

Subject I am writing on:

Websites I have approached to offer free content:

Day 30: End Your 30 Days With A Bang

What can you achieve in just one session?

Okay, go online with that list of websites that you think could be a great target for your PR. Choose one and summon it up on screen. Spend a little while digesting the layout and content of the website and then offer them a gift.

That gift could be…

A how to or informational article (ooh, what about the one that you wrote earlier) that their readers will find of interest and of value. You can offer this for free in exchange for links and a logo on their site.

Free products or sample of your services for a competition or give away.

A barter agreement where you do something for them (e.g. IT help, business advice, free samples) in exchange for coverage.

Offer them the chance to sell your product or service, either as your affiliate or under their own brand name, earning you both some money.

If there is a telephone number on the site, it is always advisable to do this in person, as this is how you build up strong relationships with your contacts. If no telephone number is listed, then an email will have to do. But do remember to personalise it, mentioning their site and your thoughts on it, to differentiate your email from spam and provoke a favourable reaction (well, hopefully).

Remember, you are offering something here for free. You are not trying to sell them anything. This distinction is very important for your own confidence and clarity when it comes to getting in touch. There's no need to be arrogant about it, just present it to them on a win win basis.

Make a note of the date that you first contacted them, and a further note in your diary to get back in contact within 5 7 days if you haven't heard anything in return.

This exercise is a great example of the best kept secret of PR   think what you can do for them, rather than what they can do for you.

Continue targeting all the websites that you have decided will be valuable for your campaign in the same way.

Summary

- Get online and give a website a present.

Day 30 Notes

Websites approached	What was offered?	Response

What Next?

I hope that you've enjoyed working your way through this workbook. If you've got a taste for attracting new clients and customers through the power of PR then you've got plenty of choices.

PR Coach

As your PR coach I work with you to increase your business revenue by attracting new clients and customers by increasing your media profile. I provide support, ideas, suggestions and PR advice as well an on going strategic look at your business and access to a structured PR programme that will equip you with all the tools and skills you need to run a successful PR campaign.

Get Noticed Consultation

This is a one off half day consultation (which takes place in London) which is a great kick start for anyone who is serious about promoting their business. I look at your business and its goals in depth and look at what you have to do, PR wise, to achieve them. I then go away and put together a six month PR and marketing strategy for you to follow, a press release for your business plus you are also enrolled on the 30 day Do Your Own PR ecourse.

Ecourses

Do Your Own PR offers a number of ecourses designed to help you get noticed and grow your business. These are:

- ✓ 30 day Do Your Own PR ecourse.
- ✓ 30 Day Promote Your Business by Writing and Selling Articles.
- ✓ 15 Build a Cult Newsletter.
- ✓ 7 Day Double Your Clients Through Networking.

✓ 15 day Write Copy that Makes People Buy
✓ 5 Day Cold Calling Crash Course.

All ecourses come with full support, feedback and a chance to brainstorm with me on ways to increase and promote your business.

Free Stuff

You can sign up for my free newsletter at

www.doyourownpr.com/subscribe.asp

The newsletter contains a PR task of the week, PR tips and advice, media requests plus details of up and coming ecourses and workshops. You can also regularly check out the PR ideas page of www.doyourownpr.com for more ideas and suggestions on steps that you can take to raise your profile. You can also bookmark the *Media Room* page where I will be posting requests from the press for interview subjects.

If you'd like to talk about any aspect of PR that this workbook has covered, or any that it hasn't, please do feel free to contact me on mail@doyourownpr.com, or speak to me on 07941 244343. I'm always happy to talk to businesses small and large on the subject of PR and it's always lovely to hear from my readers.

The very best of luck,

Paula
www.doyourownpr.com

NOTES

NOTES

NOTES

Printed in the United Kingdom
by Lightning Source UK Ltd.
109350UKS00001B/337-384